The Hitman and the Preacher

By Harold Laster

The Hit Man and the Preacher:

Copyright 2025 by Harold Laster. All rights reserved. No part of this publication may be reproduced or transmitted in any form or by any means, electronic or mechanical, including photocopy, recording, or any information storage and retrieval system, without the prior written permission of the author or publisher, except in the case of brief quotations embodied in critical articles or review. Unless otherwise indicated, all Scripture quotations are from the King James Version of the Bible.

Worldwide Kingdom Publishing 1911 Horger St.

Lincoln Park, Michigan 48146
(313) 544-8010

FIRST EDITION

ISBN: 978-1-934905-32-6

Printed in the United States of America

Acknowledgments

I want to thank the person who played a crucial role in making this book happen. Big thanks to Joyce Haddon for her helpful feedback and guidance, which really improved the manuscript. I appreciate her support, encou- ragement, and valuable contributions. This book would not have happened without you.

Dedication

To my entire Laster family,

Your constant support and encouragement have been my guiding lights during moments of inspiration and reflection. This book is dedicated to you with deep gratitude for believing in my journey and providing endless encouragement. Your presence in my life has inspired every word written on these pages.

Personal Note

I'm excited to share my latest work with you – a journey into my life and spiritual path. In these pages, you'll follow my transformation into a pastor, facing challenges and celebrating triumphs guided by unwavering faith.

As you read, I hope you find inspiration in stories of growth, resilience, and the moments that shaped my journey. It's a tale of faith, purpose, and life's twists when answering the call to serve.

Thank you for letting me share my story with you. May these pages bring reflection, encouragement, and a connection to our unique journeys.

With gratitude, HAROLD. R. LASTER

Contents

Acknowledgments ....
Dedication..
Personal Note..

Chapter 1: Roots of Resilience ....
Chapter 2: School Lessons and Early Career..........................
Chapter 3: Unveiling the Shepherd Within.............................
Chapter 4: Journey Through Struggle and Redemption..
Chapter 5: A Journey of Spiritual Awakening an Resilience...
Chapter 6: A Perilous Pursuit ....
Chapter 7: Finding Light in the Darkness...............................
Chapter 8: From Ashes to Refuge...
Chapter 9: Navigating Betrayal, Bounty, and Boundless Determination 1
Chapter 10: Family, Faith, and Finding Purpose.................... 1
Chapter 11: The Dawn of Hope... 1

Chapter 1
Roots of Resilience

As I think back on the beginning of my life, when the world just beyond our community's protective fence was rough and unfriendly, I remember those early years that shaped who I am today, carving resilience into the very fabric of my character. Imagine a time when life was hard resources were scarce, people were distant, and the struggle for survival was a constant companion. It was a landscape that tested the very core of my resilience, challenging me to find strength in the face of adversity. Amid the challenges, our community became a safe place. In the midst of chaos, relationships turned into support systems, friendships deepened into meaningful connections, and our surrogate family became the anchor that kept me steady in the storm.

As I reflect on the beginning of my existence, a time when the world just beyond the protective embrace of our community's fence was an untamed expanse, marked by rugged terrain and the unkindness that seemed to permeate the air. These formative years, characterized by harsh realities, played a pivotal role in shaping the very essence of my being. The crucible of adversity in which I found myself etched resilience into the very fabric of my character, molding me into the person I am today.

Picture a bygone era when life was an arduous journey, with resources stretched thin, distances seeming insurmountable, and the relentless struggle for survival serving as an ever- present companion. It was a landscape that demanded fortitude, a place where the indomitable spirit within me was called upon to navigate the challenges that lay ahead. In the face of scarcity and hardship, I discovered a reservoir of strength within myself that I hadn't known existed.

Yet, amid the seemingly insurmountable difficulties, our community emerged as an oasis in the midst of chaos. Within the confines of our shared haven, relationships evolved beyond mere associations—they became lifelines, intricate threads weaving a safety net against the storms of life. Friendships deepened into profound connections, each bond a testament to the resilience of the human spirit. Our surrogate family, forged through shared struggles and triumphs, became the unyielding anchor that held me steady in the tempest of existence.

In the heart of the struggle, the true beauty of human connection revealed itself. It was a time when compassion flourished, empathy thrived, and the solidarity among us illuminated the darkest corners of our shared experience. Every trial we faced was an opportunity for communal growth, an invitation to draw strength from the collective resilience of our community.

As I reminisce about those pivotal years, I am reminded of the individuals who stood alongside me, their unwavering support serving as a source of inspiration. We were bound not only by shared circumstances but by a collective determination to overcome the adversities that sought to define us. Each person in our community became a pillar of strength, a testament to the idea that, in unity, we find the fortitude to weather life's fiercest storms.

Our journey was not without its share of sacrifices. Every hardship, every setback, and every moment of despair demanded a price. Yet, in the crucible of those challenges, we discovered the transformative power of resilience. It was not a solitary endeavor; rather, it was a communal dance of perseverance, a symphony of shared resilience echoing through the annals of our collective memory.

The protective fence that once delineated the boundaries of our community became a symbol not of limitation but of collective determination. It was a reminder that, despite the harshness of the world beyond, within our enclave, we had cultivated a haven of strength and support. The fence did not confine us; it defined the sacred space where our resilience was tested and proven.

As time marched forward, the landscape beyond our community evolved, and so did we. The lessons learned in the crucible of our shared experiences continued to resonate, shaping our individual paths. The resilience etched into the very fabric of my character during those early years became a guiding force, propelling me forward even as the challenges transformed and took on new forms.

In revisiting the beginning of my life, I am confronted with a profound appreciation for the transformative power of resilience. It is a force that transcends individual struggles, weaving a common thread that binds communities together. The rugged and unkind world that once seemed daunting now stands as a testament to the resilience that resides within each of us.

In the grand story of life, the early chapters, marked by scarcity and struggle, have become a foundation upon which the rest of my narrative unfolds. The relationships forged, the bonds strengthened, and the resilience cultivated within our community continue to influence my journey, reminding me that, no matter the challenges that lie ahead, I carry within me the strength to endure and the capacity to thrive.

As I gaze back through the lens of my mind's eye, I see not just the trials endured but the triumphs celebrated, not merely the hardships faced but the resilience that emerged from the crucible of adversity. It is a story of a community that transformed challenges into opportunities, a tale of individuals who, bound by a shared commitment to resilience, weathered the storms and emerged stronger on the other side.

Recalling our family's poignant move from the comforting embrace of Alabama to the unfamiliar chill of Michigan stirs up memories of a significant turning point. Fueled by audacious hopes for a better life, my indomitable mother, shouldering the responsibility of eight kids while Dad served gallantly in the military, gracefully led us through a transformative journey marked by sacrifice, unyielding determination, and the relentless pursuit of improvement.

A central pillar of our hard-earned stability was the rhythm of Mom's cleaning job. With every measured sweep of the floor and every meticulously folded piece of laundry, she showcased her unwavering efforts, becoming an enduring beacon that taught me the enduring values of hard work and resilience from the tenderest of ages.

In the unlikeliest of corners, I discovered

unexpected role models - the enigmatic figures of pimps and those orchestrating after-hours joints. Surprisingly, their accepting nature provided a sanctuary where I could genuinely be myself, and amidst adversity, their unexpected support played a substantial role in shaping the unique contours of my journey.

In the story I unfold, a cascade of emotions, ranging from the palpable fear of the unknown to the tangible hope that guided our every step, weaves through the narrative. Each moment unfolds as a delicate brushstroke, contributing to the rich mosaic of my struggles and triumphs.

The journey from the comforting familiarity of Alabama to the uncharted territory of Michigan meant confronting fears of the unknown, adapting to a new place, and adeptly managing a burgeoning list of responsibilities. Yet, intricately woven with fear was the radiant thread of hope, a gentle light that steadfastly guided our determination to overcome the formidable challenges that lay ahead.

Despair lingered, a persistent shadow threatening to engulf us as we navigated the weight of newfound responsibilities, acclimated to unfamiliar surroundings, and confronted the relentless demands of daily life. But from the depths of adversity, determination emerged as an unwavering force, propelling us forward with resilience that defied the odds.

My experiences intertwine to form a complex mosaic, where each challenge met with unyielding resilience contributes to the intricate patterns of my journey. Triumphs, akin to bursts of vibrant color on a canvas, marked our achievements, adding depth and vibrancy to the evolving masterpieces of our lives.

As time passed, our journey's emotional landscape shifted. Fear turned into a sense of belonging, hope transformed into opportunities, and despair gave way to resilie

nce. Adversity, met with determination, became a catalyst for growth.

Reflecting on our family's journey, I see that the emotions in those moments shaped my character and painted the canvas of my identity. The move from Alabama to Michigan was not just a change in location but a transformative experience that molded the person I am today.

In summary, our family's transition from Alabama to Michigan wasn't just about moving places; it was a journey that sculpted my character. Motivated by dreams of a better life, my mother's determination was the driving force behind our collective resilience. Through sacrifices and successes, the emotions that colored our experiences formed a vivid tapestry—a testament to the power of resilience and the enduring spirit that defines our unique journey.

Thinking back on the early parts of my

life and looking at them closely helps me understand things better. Reflecting on my past, I see how fate and my choices mixed together.

The community, once just around me, becomes a crucial place where my character gets stronger. It acts like a shield, keeping out the tough stuff from the outside world, a safe space where my ability to bounce back grows.

In my life's intricate design, being tough isn't just one thing; it's a mix of experiences, relationships, and having inner strength. It's about finding strength in places I didn't expect, building up toughness through tough times with others, and facing the hard parts of growing up with grit and honesty.

As the story starts, it's not just a look back; it's the beginning of a journey where my strength, planted in tough times, goes deep inside me. This chapter isn't just remembering what happened; it's saying loud and clear that my ability to bounce back will be with me in the future—a sign of the unbeatable spirit shaped by my early years.

In this ongoing story, thinking about the past isn't only about what already happened, but it's a way to understand things now and in the days to come. The community, now seen as a place that helps me become strong, keeps playing a big part in making me who I am.

As the story of being tough goes on, it shows how different things—lessons from unexpected teachers, the friendships formed in hard times, and being true to myself in tough situations—all fit together. Every part of this complex picture adds to the story, showing a toughness that changes, learns, and keeps getting stronger.

This journey isn't just about going in one direction; it's like going in circles, exploring what being tough means. The start, where I declared my toughness, echoes through the later stories, like a strong beat in the pages of my life. The tough times from my past stay with me, shaping and making my spirit stronger as I keep going through life's unknown paths.

Chapter 2

School Lessons and Early Career

As I navigated through my early years, I discovered that true strength arises from heeding the wisdom passed down through generations. It's not merely about blindly adhering to rules; rather, it involves recognizing the valuable insights awaiting those who listen. This realization ignited my curiosity and eagerness for knowledge.

In my teenage years, I often dreamt of becoming a policeman or firefighter, inspired by exciting stories from older folks. Those tales filled me with a sense of adventure. However, life had different plans for me, leading me to explore new possibilities beyond the usual paths. This brought a mix of uncertainty and curiosity more independent, although it also brought a mix of excitement and nervousness. Each job taught me about sticking to commitments, staying organized, and working hard. Overall, these experiences helped me become more self-sufficient and gave me a real sense of accomplishment.

In my formative years, Mr. Cooley became a significant mentor. He employed a blend of tough love to shape my character and instruct me on overcoming challenges. I admired him, experiencing a mix of respect and a touch of apprehension. Beyond standard lessons, he demonstrated how to navigate life's obstacles, offering solace during difficult moments and guiding me through uncertainties.

Every experience, each shift guided by a divine calling, played a part in crafting the intricate design of my life—a journey defined by growth, strength, and purpose. This has left me with a deep sense of fulfillment and excitement for the adventures that lie ahead.

I was really intimidated by him. He was an older man, probably in his 60s, and came to school every day with his wife driving him. He seemed serious and rarely smiled, making me feel nervous around him.

His focus on excellence within our mostly black community deeply connected with me, fostering a sense of responsibility and deter- mination. He emphasized the importance of being sharp, on point, and well-educated, igniting both a drive to succeed and a fear of not meeting his expectations.

Even though he had a strict way of doing things, he made it clear that his aim was to help us become better people. Occasionally, he showed genuine care and concern, softening his strict approach. He admitted he would expect a lot from us, but he genuinely cared about our success, making me feel both respectful and a bit nervous. He said being strict was needed to bring us up to the required standard so we could do well in tests and be competitive. This left me feeling a strong sense of urgency and determination to meet his expectations.

Mr. Cooley made a memorable entrance, arriving in an older limousine driven by his wife, which added to his sense of authority and grabbed our attention. As he got out, he quickly explained his teaching style, exuding confidence that both daunted and motivated me. His pledge to go through every test in class was both comforting and challenging, backed by a promise to teach us the material thoroughly. Yet, with this assurance came a serious warning – not meeting his expectations would result in quick and unwavering discipline. This made me determined to meet the challenges he set.

Under his rules, boys and girls risked getting physically punished for any mistakes, like failing a test or not doing homework. This made the classroom feel tense and anxious. He used a big paddle for discipline, not showing favoritism based on gender. This created a strong fear of punishment that hung over us like a dark cloud.

This kind of "tough love" had a big impact, like the "scared straight" method used in youth justice to discourage criminal behavior. It left us feeling torn between being upset and reluctantly recognizing its effectiveness. Even though Mr. Cooley's discipline initially made us angry and embarrassed, it was clear that he treated everyone fairly and had a noticeable effect on how well we did in school. This made us face our mistakes and work harder to avoid punishment.

While his methods may have caused some controversy and discomfort, the clear improve- ments in grades and overall performance spoke loudly about how effective his approach was. This left us with a reluctant respect for the man who pushed us to be our best selves, even if it meant confronting our fears.

Thinking back on those formative years, I juggled various responsibilities, handling finances from a young age to support myself and even buy gifts for my grandmother. This early journey into responsible adulthood was shaped by Mr. Cooley's influence and the lessons learned in his classroom, putting me on a path toward success and independence from a surprisingly young age.

My encounters with Mr. Cooley paved the way for me to introduce another significant person in my life: Deacon Modoc, my brother-in-law. Despite a noticeable age difference of 15 years between him and my sister, Deacon Modock seamlessly became a wise elder in our family. His impact on my life was profound, particularly after my time under Mr. Cooley's guidance.

I ended up staying with Deacon Modoc due to my troublesome behavior, which had become a cause for concern for my mother. Engaging in late- night activities and other inappropriate behaviors made my family believe that his disciplined approach could positively influence my conduct. Indeed, it did. Despite being strict, Deacon Modoc's guidance played a crucial role in shaping my character, instilling valuable lessons about responsibility and manhood in me.

His influence extended beyond mere discipline; Deacon Modoc actively facilitated my personal development, helping me secure employment and manage various aspects of my life. Under his roof, academic excellence was non- negotiable—I was expected to maintain a minimum grade of a C. Living with my loving sister further enriched my experience, as she provided unwavering support and guidance, stepping into the role of a mentor.

One incident vividly illustrates Deacon Modoc's unwavering character during a journey from Detroit to California in his mobile home. Encountering a group of Hell's Angels Motorcycle Club members whose disruptive behavior had escalated tensions, Deacon Modoc fearlessly took charge of the situation. Despite the potentially intimidating circumstances, he remained steadfast and resolute, navigating the mobile home through the chaos with unwavering determination.

Even in the face of advice from my sister to consider the potential risks, Deacon Modoc remained undeterred. The timely intervention of law enforcement ultimately diffused the situation, preventing any escalation of hostilities from the motorcycle club.

In that intense moment, when tension gripped the air, Deacon Modoc's bravery made a lasting impression on me. His unwavering courage inspired a sense of fearlessness, shaping who I am. As I grew up and eventually joined the military, I found that same strength within myself, thanks to Deacon Modoc's example.

Even now, I carry this fearlessness with me. I'm not afraid to face a crowd or confront someone who means harm. This enduring quality comes from the strong spirit I saw in Deacon Modock and made my own.

Something inside me now refuses to give in to fear, authority, or intimidation. Thanks to my brother-in-law's influence, I can face any situation with confidence and determination. His bravery taught me how to tackle life's challenges head-on.

His resilience was evident in every situation. He didn't hesitate to confront the culprits when our home was broken into during a church trip. His words, backed by his readiness to protect us, showed me how to stand up against adversity.

This resilience was especially evident when our family faced threats from dangerous individuals. Drawing on the strength and courage I learned from Deacon Modock, I stood firm in the face of danger. Even though he's no longer with us, his lessons and bravery continue to guide me.

Chapter 3

Unveiling the Shepherd Within

The air buzzed with tension as the sun dipped low, casting long shadows on our Detroit street. I will never forget that day, the soldiers striding down the road in their intimidating uniforms, rifles at the ready position. They were shouting a name, their voices echoing off the worn buildings. Everyone knew why they were there.

It was all because of a love deemed taboo by society—a young man involved with a white girl. The soldiers were there to punish him for daring to cross racial lines; their mission was clear as day.

Their presence sent shivers down our spines, and fear gripped the neighborhood. It was a sight that left me feeling a mix of anger, sadness, and fear for my community's safety.

Faced with such a threat, I felt compelled to protect myself and those I cared about. So, I took matters into my own hands and crafted a ZIP gun—a makeshift weapon made from wood and a car antenna.

With each carve and assembly, I silently promised to defend my loved ones against the chaos outside. Holding the finished product, I knew I was ready to stand up against the storm of hatred and oppression. Love and defiance would be our strongest allies.

At just nine years old, I found myself holding a gun—a stark symbol of the danger lurking in our Detroit neighborhood, brought on by the presence of Klansmen. It's hard to forget that feeling—the mix of fear and responsibility that weighed heavy on my young shoulders.

The thought of a kid like me having to protect his family felt like something out of a movie. But this was real life, and there was no script to follow. I was just a kid trying to make sense of a world that seemed determined to tear us apart from the moment we entered it.

I remember the day those Klansmen marched down our street like something out of a nightmare. There must have been about thirty of them dressed up like soldiers with rifles slung over their shoulders. Their voices rang out, calling for someone by name—a man they wanted to hurt just because of who he loved.

It was terrifying, watching them from the window as they stomped down the street, filling the air with their hate and anger. My mom pulled me away, her voice urgent and scared, telling me to stay out of sight.

But even inside, I could feel the tension thick in the air, like a storm about to break. It was a moment that stayed with me, a reminder of the dangers we faced just for being who we were. And yet, even in the face of that fear, there was a stubborn kind of hope—a belief that somehow, someway, we would make it through.

One day, as the sun was beginning its descent, casting a warm golden glow that danced through the aisles of the grocery store where I toiled away my days. I had finally finished my shift, was weary but determined, and stepped out into the cool evening air; I felt relief. Another day, I survived in a world that often felt like it was stacked against me.

But my moment of respite was short-lived. Just as I reached the threshold of the store, four looming figures materialized before me—police officers, their presence casting a shadow over the tranquility of the evening. They were known as the Big Four, a name that carried weight in the hearts and minds of all who called Michigan home.

As they approached, the air crackled with tension, their expressions stern and unyielding. It was a scene that played out all too often in the streets of our city—a reminder of the ever-present threat of authority, poised to assert its power over those deemed unworthy in the eyes of society.

But there was something about these particular officers that sent a chill down my spine and set my heart racing. They were not just any police officers; they were the embodiment of fear and intimidation, their very presence a harbinger of trouble.

And trouble, it seemed, was exactly what they had in mind. With a sense of purpose that left no room for doubt, they descended upon me, their hands reaching for the tools of their trade—cuffs, batons, the implements of oppression.

But even as they moved to detain me, I refused to cower in the face of their authority, for I knew that I was not alone, that there were others who had come before me, who had stared down the barrel of injustice and refused to back down.

And so, as the Big Four closed in around me, I stood my ground, my heart pounding in my chest, a silent prayer on my lips. For in that moment, I knew that I was not just fighting for myself but for all those who had been silenced by the heavy hand of oppression.

Without warning, they descended upon me, their blows raining down with a ferocity that left me reeling. The harsh glare of their flashlights illuminated the alley, casting twisted shadows against the brick walls as I dropped to my knees, the pain blossoming like a wildfire in my chest.

When I stood up, the policeman began

beating me, using long flashlights. They struck me with the back of the flashlights 20 times. Something inside of me felt like God's hands took away all the pain. Despite appearing to cry, I felt no pain due to the hand of God.

It was a scene that played out all too often in the streets of our city—a reminder of the ever- present threat of authority, poised to assert its power over those deemed unworthy in the eyes of society.

And yet, even in the midst of my suffering, my mind wandered back to another moment, a memory etched into the fabric of my being. I was just a boy of fourteen, fresh out of junior high, when a man approached me with a knife, his intentions clear as day.

But then, like a guardian angel, my brother appeared. He had returned from Vietnam, his uniform a symbol of courage and strength in the face of adversity. He disarmed the man with a single swift motion, sending him fleeing into the night.

At that moment, as I looked into my brother's eyes, gratitude and relief washing over me like a wave, I knew that I was not alone. For no matter how dark the night may seem, there was always a glimmer of hope—a beacon of light to guide me through the darkness.

The devil's relentless pursuit to snuff out my life has been a recurring theme, a haunting melody that has echoed through the years with chilling persistence. He has wielded every tool at his disposal, manipulating those around me in a twisted game of chess where my very existence hangs in the balance.

It wasn't until much later in life that I began to unravel the enigma of my existence to understand the role I was destined to play in this cosmic battle between good and evil. From the tender age of five, when I first set foot in the hallowed halls of education, I found myself thrust into a role I had not yet grasped—the role of a shepherd, a protector of the weak and vulnerable.

At the heart of being a pastor is a deeper purpose—it's a calling, a divine invitation from God Himself. It's not just about picking a job; it's about embracing a higher mission, a sacred responsibility to serve others and share His message.

Similar to any profession, being a pastor requires the right attitude and a mix of kindness, understanding, and unwavering belief. It's not for the faint-hearted; it's for those who feel compelled to guide and uplift others through life's challenges.

For many starting out in ministry, the journey begins with God's guidance—a mentorship under the Divine, whose presence lights the way. I remember my first role, working alongside the all- knowing Shepherd, whose wisdom and kindness made a lasting impression on me.

Under His guidance, I learned that being a pastor goes beyond words and rituals. It's about being a beacon of hope in a world full of uncertainty, a source of comfort for those in need.

My Mentor taught me that being a pastor is a sacred promise, a commitment to walk alongside others through their joys and sorrows. Through His example, I understood that this calling isn't just a job; it's a divine calling given by God Himself.

I became a pastor before I knew what it meant to pastor, and my innate sense of compassion guided me as I cared for those who could not care for themselves. Whether it was ensuring that hungry children had enough to eat at school or finding ways to provide for the less fortunate, I was always there, a beacon of hope in a world consumed by darkness.

But as I grew older, I began to see the cracks in my façade, the flaws that lurked beneath the surface of my seemingly noble intentions. I was not a good pastor, not in the truest sense of the word. For a while I may have provided for the physical needs of those around me, however I neglected the deeper, more spiritual aspects of my calling.

It was a harsh realization that cut me to the core and left me questioning everything I thought I knew about myself. How could I claim to be a shepherd of souls when I couldn't even find solace in my own heart? How could I lead others to salvation when I was lost in the wilderness of my doubt and fear?

But even in the midst of my despair, I clung to a glimmer of hope—a belief that redemption was possible, that I could rise above my shortcomings and become the pastor I was always meant to be. So, with renewed determination and a humble heart, I set out on a journey of self- discovery, seeking forgiveness for my past transgressions and striving to become the man I was destined to be.

The devil tried to kill me time and time, again and again, year after year, but he could never extinguish the flame of hope that burned within me. As I continue on this journey, I know that with faith as my guide, I will emerge from the shadows stronger, wiser, and more resolute than ever before.

Chapter 4

Journey Through Struggle and Redemption

At 17, my journey into adulthood took an unconventional turn as I enlisted in the military. Little did I know then that this decision would sculpt my character and define my path forward. The military was not just about combat and discipline; it was a transformative experience that instilled in me the values I carry today.

Amidst the rigorous training routines, one aspect stood out, marksmanship. The firing range became my classroom, and the instructors, my mentors. I vividly recall the sense of achievement as I honed my skills, becoming the second best shooter in my regiment. It wasn't just about hitting targets; it was about discipline, precision, and the responsibility that came with wielding such power.

Hand-to-hand combat training further solidified my capabilities, turning me into a well- rounded soldier. Yet, beyond the physical aspect, the military instilled in me a deeper understanding of leadership. As a squad leader, I guided my comrades through challenges, fostered camara- derie, and led by example.

However, one particular experience left a lasting impression amidst the drills and camaraderie. It was the story of a young recruit, hailing from a vastly different background than most of us. His journey mirrored the diversity of our nation, reflecting the rich tapestry of experiences within the military.

As I reflect on those formative years, I

realize that the military was not just about learning how to fight; it was about learning how to lead, adapt, and embrace diversity. These principles, ingrained in me during my time in service, continue to shape my approach to life, guiding me through its myriad challenges and triumphs.

They beckoned me relentlessly, calling out my name time and again. This relentless summoning was labeled a "blanket party," a term born from his persistent refusal to maintain personal hygiene or cleanliness, inevitably leading us to fail inspections.

In an act of collective frustration, some individuals took matters into their own hands. They swiftly covered him with a blanket, concealing his identity, and proceeded to deliver blows, wielding makeshift weapons fashioned from socks filled with soap. This, in the military, was what they termed a blanket party.

Though I was not present during this incident, the story swiftly circulated through the ranks, whispered among those who bore witness. As a squad leader, I returned to find myself facing the consequences. Military police awaited me, locking me up without explanation.

Confounded, I questioned their actions, vehemently asserting my innocence. How could I be held accountable for an event I had no part in? These fellow soldiers of my background were meant to be allies, yet their actions resulted in unjust repercussions for me. The military punished me with a 30-day confinement without pay despite my protests of innocence.

The black folks promised, saying they would visit me and be there for me, claiming we were friends, like brothers. However, one big lesson I learned then, and still carry with me today, is that those same folks never showed up. Even during my 30 days in jail, they did not visit me or write a single letter. They just moved on, leaving me behind bars.

I stayed quiet even when I could have snitched on them to get out.

The captain in charge of us came by, though. He suggested I spill the beans on those guys to get out. But I stuck to my story, telling him I was not involved. He explained that I could not let them off easy as a squad leader. I reminded him I was not even there. After 30 days, when he saw I wouldn't rat them out, he came back and told me they were dropping all charges. Knowing my loyalty paid off, even if it meant spending time in jail, was a relief.

They told me they were giving me back pay for the month and that I could go. But they also made sure to impart a crucial life lesson. They said, "You can't trust people just because they are black like you." Friendship runs deeper than skin color. The captain asked if those folks ever visited or wrote to me. I shook my head. "No," I replied.

He pointed out that these were the same

people I was protecting. I argued back, saying I was not covering for them; I just couldn't bring myself to be part of something I was not involved in. That lesson stuck with me, even now. I've come to understand that not everyone who comes your way is a true friend. You cannot be friends with bad or racist people. It was a lesson learned in the military that I still carry with me.

When I returned home, I crossed paths with a young man named Charles. He thought highly of me and thought his sister might, too. He suggested I meet her, so we headed to his house. Upstairs, his sister awaited, and when she descended, I was struck by her beauty like none other I'd seen before. We exchanged words, and she kindly offered me a ham sandwich from the kitchen. We sat together on the couch, munching away.

In the first 15 minutes of meeting her, I couldn't help but blurt out, "I'm going to marry you." She laughed, thinking I was joking. But to me, she was everything I'd ever dreamed of. Despite my earnestness, she brushed it off as playful banter.

However, fate had other plans. Within a few months, while on leave, I found myself in a car accident on the freeway. Another driver rear-ended my car, leaving me injured.

After the accident, I was in bad shape. She thought I was joking about marrying her, but I meant every word. Within two to three months, while I was home on leave, the accident occurred. I was on the freeway when a guy rear-ended my car, leaving me seriously injured. I was passing out, dizzy whenever I stood up, yet unaware of the extent of my injuries.

Despite my condition, I was determined to marry the woman who is now my wife. But no one sympathized because I was deemed too young for marriage; I had to be 21. So, reluctantly, I had to return to the military, back to Germany. From afar, I continued to write to her, sending pictures and promising that when I returned, we'd marry.

When I returned to the United States, I reunited with my wife. We didn't rush into marriage; instead, we spent a year or so together before tying the knot. Until then, I'd never experienced love like this, and even now, she remains the only one I've ever loved.

After marrying my wife, I found myself falling in with a troublesome crowd. These were people from my childhood, friends from the old neighborhood. I had known them since I was eight or nine years old, but things had changed. They were involved in drugs, though I wasn't initially. Yet, as I spent more time with them, I found myself getting involved in drugs, too. Before long, I was caught in a downward spiral, dragged into a world I never thought I'd find myself in.

After getting hooked on drugs, I found

myself walking 15 miles in the dead of night just to feed my addiction. I traversed through dimly lit alleyways, knowing exactly when the police shifts changed and when they were patrolling. With every step, I scoured for anything I could steal and sell to get my fix. It was a descent into darkness, where I navigated the night with an animalistic instinct, unseen by those around me who wandered obliviously.

I became adept at moving silently, a skill I honed from my military training. I moved with such stealth that even the dogs remained silent as I passed by. In those moments, I embodied a different kind of existence, where silence and stealth were my allies in pursuing my next high.

I never realized the significance of moving in silence until it saved my life one fateful day. The lessons I learned during my darkest times battling addiction ended up becoming the lifeline for my family. It was a revelation that I had not anticipated that God would utilize the darkest shadows of my existence to bring light and salvation to my loved ones, keeping us alive against all odds.

For about a year, I traversed those 15 miles, navigating the labyrinthine alleyways in pursuit of my next fix. Little did I know that my routine journey home in the dead of night would coincide with a pivotal moment in my life.

As I made my way home one early morning, the rain poured down relentlessly, each raindrop feeling like a heavy weight upon my weary shoulders. I was soaked to the bone, the water seeping through my clothes down to my very skin. Yet, it was as if the rain itself carried a message, washing away the haze of addiction that clouded my judgment.

With each step closer to home, I felt the weight of the rain not just on my body but on my soul. Looking up to the heavens, raindrops pelted my face, almost as if nature was urging me to speak up and reach out to the divine.

At that moment, with raindrops stinging my eyes, I found myself engaging in a conversation with God, speaking aloud into the darkness. I pleaded with Him, recalling how He had intervened in my mother's life, pulling her out of the grips of alcoholism.

I raised my voice to the heavens, the rain mixing with my tears as I cried out to God. "Look at me, God," I implored, my words echoing into the night. "See what I have become, wandering these streets in the darkness."

Each step through the rain-soaked alleys felt heavier than the last, burdened by the weight of my drenched clothes and the heaviness of my soul. The darkness around me mirrored the turmoil within, a stark contrast to the flickering streetlights that struggled to penetrate the shadows.

Yet, even amid the downpour, I felt a

glimmer of hope stirring within me. It was as if the rain, relentless in its descent, carried with it a message of renewal and redemption. With each raindrop that kissed my skin, I felt a cleansing power washing over me, washing away the stains of my past mistakes.

Chapter 5

A Journey of Spiritual Awakening and Resilience

Living in the darkness of night, I felt caught up in a plea for help, like when my mom was miraculously saved. As I prayed hard, begging for God to step in, my cries became louder and more desperate. It felt like I was being driven by some unseen force, my words shifting into a language I could not understand. Yet, there was an unmistakable power behind them.

Even though I wanted to stop speaking that strange language, I could not. Every time I tried to head home, it's like I was stuck in a confusing maze of words. The door, hidden in the dark, feels like a scary obstacle.

Feeling sad and panicky, I knock on the door, the sound echoing in the quiet night. My wife's worried voice broke through my strange speech, asking who was there. But I could not answer in words she'd understood, only later realizing it was some kind of special language that had taken over me.

It was a moment of divine intervention as if tongues of fire from God descended upon me. Despite my attempts to explain to my wife that it was still me, her husband, she could not comprehend my words. Instead, she found herself swept up in the same mystical language that had enveloped me. As she embraced me at the door, the transformative power of God surged through my being.

I felt it deep within as if a blazing inferno raged between my skin and my bones. The intensity was overwhelming, a searing heat that coursed from the crown of my head down to the very soles of my feet. It was a sensation both glorious and consuming, leaving me ablaze with the fervor of divine presence.

My wife, sensing the magnitude of the moment, reached for the phone. With a sense of urgency and reverence, she conveyed to my mother the miraculous occurrence unfolding before her eyes. Explaining that I was speaking in tongues of fire, she ignited a chain reaction of spiritual connection.

Across the city of Michigan, the flames of this sacred language spread, engulfing hearts and minds in a transcendent communion. From household to household, the divine tongues echoed, uniting souls in a symphony of faith and devotion. It was a testament to the boundless power of God's love, igniting a wildfire of spiritual awakening throughout the land.

As the news of my salvation spread like wildfire through the community, a chorus of rejoicing voices echoed in its wake. Friends, family, and neighbors reached out to one another, sharing the miraculous turn of events that had transpired in my life. Before the morning sun had fully risen, however, the adversary himself sought to test my newfound resolve.

A call from the drug dealer I had distanced myself from served as a stark reminder of the darkness that still lingered on the fringes of my past. Accusing me of a crime I had not committed, he threatened my very existence with chilling certainty. But in that moment of confrontation, I stood firm, fortified by the newfound faith that burned within me.

"I did not trespass into your domain," I asserted with unwavering conviction. "I stand within the sanctity of my home, sheltered by the With a courage born of faith, I challenged him to confront me directly, relinquishing all weapons and defenses. "If you seek my demise," I declared boldly, "then come and face me without deceit or subterfuge. I shall await you on my porch, unguarded and unafraid."

Turning to my brother-in-law for assistance, I swiftly disarmed myself, relinquishing any semblance of retaliation or aggression. As I awaited the confrontation, a sense of peace washed over me, for I knew that in the face of darkness, the light of divine protection shone brightest.

After sending my wife away for safety, I remained perched on the porch, a lone sentinel amidst the quiet hum of suburban life. Hours stretched into eternity as I awaited the con- frontation that never materialized. The drug dealer, once a looming specter of menace, faded into the shadows of memory, never to darken my doorstep again.

As the sun dipped below the horizon and stars emerged in the velvet sky, I found solace in the stillness, a tangible reassurance of divine protection. From that pivotal moment, my life took on a new trajectory, guided by the guiding light of faith.

With a renewed sense of purpose, I made my way to the Pentecostal Temple, where the doors of salvation had opened wide to welcome the lost and weary. It was there, within the hallowed halls of the church, that I found redemption and was welcomed into the fold of believers.

In the years that followed, I embarked on a journey of spiritual growth and enlightenment, attending ministerial classes offered by the church. These classes, meticulously designed to equip aspiring ministers with the knowledge and skills needed for their sacred calling, became the cornerstone of my transformation.

Under the guidance of seasoned mentors and fellow seekers of truth, I delved into the scriptures, honed my oratorical skills, and cultivated a deep understanding of the tenets of faith.

As my fellow ministers underwent rigorous testing and examination to validate their calling, I, too, prepared diligently and eager to demonstrate my unwavering commitment to serving the Lord. When the time came to stand before the board and profess my faith, I did so with humility and conviction, knowing that I had been called to a higher purpose.

The ministerial training at our church was a transformative experience that spanned several months, equipping us with the knowledge and skills necessary to serve as ambassadors of faith. Under the guidance of esteemed teachers like Minister Graham and Pastor Laster, the classes delved deep into scripture, theology, and pastoral care.

As aspiring ministers, we dedicated ourselves to the rigorous curriculum, attending lectures, participating in discussions, and immersing ourselves in prayer and worship. The training was not just about academic knowledge; it was about nurturing a profound spiritual connection and developing the character traits essential for effective ministry.

Throughout the training, we were reminded of the importance of obtaining our ministerial license—a validation of our calling and a formal recognition of our readiness to serve. This license represented more than just a piece of paper; it symbolized our commitment to upholding the values and principles of our faith community.

For me, the impact of this training extended far beyond the classroom. It was a journey of personal growth and spiritual awakening. It strengthened my relationship with God, deepened my understanding of scripture, and instilled within me a sense of purpose and mission.

Armed with the knowledge and authority conferred by my ministerial license, I embarked on a new chapter of my life, ready to minister to the spiritual needs of others and spread the message of hope and redemption.

It was a calling I embraced wholeheartedly, knowing that through faith and dedication, I could make a meaningful difference in the lives of those around me.

In reflecting on my ministerial training, the names of the teachers and pastors who guided me stand out vividly. Note that I finished my training correspondence WITH BISHOP LEE. H EVANS. Equally influential was Pastor Laster, my older brother, whose leadership and mentorship shaped my spiritual journey in profound ways. His dynamic preaching stirred my soul, challenging me to delve deeper into scripture and confront the truths it held. One sermon, in particular, resonated deeply with me—the message of resilience in the face of adversity.

It was during these moments of reflection that I realized the true significance of my calling. While obtaining a ministerial license may seem trivial to some, for me, it symbolized a com- mitment to stand firm in the face of adversity and proclaim the gospel message without fear or hesitation.

However, amidst the academic rigors of training, it was the trials and tribulations of life that truly tested my faith and resolve. The attempts on my life by the forces of darkness, the relentless pursuit of evil seeking to extinguish the light within me. These were the moments that defined my ministry.

In a world where violence and chaos threaten the sanctity of our sacred spaces, we must confront the harsh realities of spiritual warfare. I hope that through my experiences, recounted in these pages, readers will gain a deeper understanding of the spiritual battles that rage unseen and find solace in the knowledge that even in the darkest of times, the light of faith can prevail. The devil, always lurking in the shadows, seeks to sow chaos and discord in my life, manifesting through the challenges I face with my children and my wife. Amidst this turmoil, the significance of a minister's license pales in comparison.

From the earliest days of my existence, I was unwittingly fulfilling the role of a pastor, shepherding others with a divine calling that transcended earthly credentials. There were no official licenses or certificates; I was simply born into this sacred duty.

The formalities of training and licensure held little sway over my journey. It was the profound encounter with Bishop Evans, following a life-altering incident overseas, that bestowed upon me the recognition of my calling. Yet, even before the ink dried on my license, tragedy struck with the shooting of my wife, shaking me from my spiritual bearings.

Since that pivotal moment, the forces of darkness have relentlessly pursued me, seeking to snuff out the light of my newfound faith. Yet, despite the ever-present threat, I have forged ahead, driven by an unwavering determination to defy the enemy's schemes.

In the wake of my salvation, my life underwent a radical transformation. With divine guidance, I established two successful companies—Sure Shot Pest Control and Star Tire—propelled by a newfound clarity of purpose and direction. These ventures flourished, expanding beyond my wildest dreams, a testament to the abundance that flowed from my newfound connection with the divine.

My mind, once clouded by doubt and uncertainty, now brims with the confidence and vision of a true entrepreneur. The enemy, recognizing the threat posed by my burgeoning success, has launched relentless attacks aimed at undermining my prosperity.

Yet, despite the adversities that beset me, I remain steadfast in my faith, knowing that the same power that transformed my life continues to guide and protect me. Even my wife, once on the verge of leaving, now stands by my side, a testament to the miraculous changes wrought by the hand of God.

Chapter 6

A Perilous Pursuit

As time flowed like a river, swift yet transformative, a new chapter unfolded in the narrative of my life. In the span of mere months, what felt like a year's worth of progress blossomed before my eyes.

Since the moment of salvation, a remarkable evolution has taken root within me. With determination as my compass, I ventured into the realm of property ownership, each acquisition a testament to my unwavering resolve. Cash transactions became the norm as I navigated the landscape of investments with newfound confidence.

Amidst this whirlwind of growth, the

trappings of success began to manifest in tangible ways. Behind the wheel of brand-new cars, I embarked on journeys that symbolized not just mobility but the fruits of relentless labor and dedication.

As the doors of our church swung open to welcome seekers of solace and faith, they were met not only with the warmth of fellowship but with tangible evidence of prosperity. The sight of a pristine vehicle parked within our sanctuary served as a beacon of hope, a tangible reminder that dreams were not merely spoken but brought to fruition within these walls.

In my new life, the ladies of the church became like family to me. They taught me so much, and I wanted to show appreciation. Whenever I could, I would slip a little money into their purses, which they left open for me on purpose. Their smiles and homemade cakes were a constant source of joy.

These older ladies, some in their 50s and

60s, treated me like royalty. They were always there for me, showering me with love and attention. It was heartwarming and beautiful.

As my wife and I delved deeper into our roles as ministers, we attended classes for years, and it paid off. I was recognized as the top soul winner of the year, bringing more people into the church than anyone else. They even gave me a trophy, proudly displayed at the Mother Church.

One day, after collecting rent, my wife and I found ourselves on 8th Mile, browsing furniture stores. As my wife and I browsed through furniture, our cozy mobile home parked nearby, a van pulled up behind us, casting an ominous shadow over our day. Through the rearview mirror, I watched as rough-looking men, some black, some white, stepped out, armed with rifles. Fear gripped me as I pulled my wife away, but before we could escape, they closed in.

Suddenly, shots rang out, shattering the peaceful scene. I watched in horror as bullets tore through our vehicle, hitting my wife and narrowly missing me. Her screams pierced the chaos as we sped away, the sound of gunfire echoing in our ears.

In the aftermath, as we caught our breath, I could not shake the image of my wife's pain and the bullet lodged in the headrest where I had been sitting. It was a moment of sheer terror that left us shaken to our core, grateful to be alive but forever changed by the violence that had erupted so unexpectedly.

With adrenaline coursing through my veins, I instinctively shielded my wife's trembling form with my own, hunching down in the seat of our vehicle as we rolled hurriedly down the street. Despite the chaos erupting around us, the only thought that occupied my mind was to keep moving, to put as much distance as possible between us and the assailants.

In a stroke of providence, an off-duty police officer appeared on the scene, a beacon of hope amidst the turmoil. Though he lacked the means to confront the armed aggressors, he diligently recorded the license plate number of the vehicle responsible for the attack. It was a small gesture of assistance, tinged with the palpable fear of retribution, as the long rifles wielded by our assailants cast a shadow of intimidation.

With a sense of urgency propelling us forward, we navigated the streets with a singular focus, our destination clear: the hospital. The journey seemed interminable, every passing moment fraught with uncertainty and fear for my wife's well-being.

Upon our arrival at the receiving hospital, a sense of relief washed over me as medical personnel sprang into action, tending to my wounded wife with practiced efficiency. The sight of her injury, a gunshot wound to the leg, sent a shiver down my spine. Yet, the absence of crimson blood was a perplexing sight, replaced instead by a strange, clear liquid tinged with hues of pink. It was a stark reminder of the surreal nature of our ordeal, a stark departure from the familiar crimson of human blood.

As the medical staff tended to my wife's physical wounds, I found myself grappling with the emotional toll of the experience. In the quiet moments that followed, I turned to my wife, seeking solace and understanding in the wake of our brush with mortality. With trembling words, I posed the question that lingered heavily in the air: What had transpired to bring us to this moment of peril?

As the shock of the attack began to wane, a torrent of questions flooded our minds, each more haunting than the last. Why had we been targeted? Was it a simple robbery gone awry or something far more sinister—a contract hit, perhaps, orchestrated with malicious intent? The uncertainty gnawed at us, leaving us grappling for answers in the aftermath of the harrowing ordeal.

As we retraced the events leading up to the shooting, doubts and suspicions loomed large. Had I unknowingly crossed paths with someone from my past, igniting a vendetta that had culminated in violence? The weight of such conjecture hung heavy in the air, casting a pall over our once- peaceful existence.

Yet, amidst the turmoil of unanswered questions, life marched on. Our burgeoning wealth seemed to eclipse all else as my company flourished, driving competitors out of business and securing lucrative city contracts with alarming efficiency. The Three-Way Keel Method, a breakthrough in pest control, became a citywide phenomenon, propelling our company to new heights of success.

Blinded by ambition and driven by the promise of prosperity, I failed to recognize the collateral damage left in our wake. The very growth that fueled our ascent inadvertently deprived others of their livelihoods, siphoning food from their children's mouths. The magnitude of our impact began to dawn on us, a sobering realization that our success came at a cost—one we had never intended to bear.

As our company garnered attention and accolades, we found ourselves thrust into the spotlight, featured on television, and hailed as entrepreneurial trailblazers. Yet, behind the veneer of success lurked a darker truth: our prosperity had come at the expense of others' well-being, unwittingly sowing the seeds of animosity and resentment.

Unbeknownst to us, our actions had provoked ire and resentment among those we had unwittingly displaced and disadvantaged. Checks from the government, once a symbol of triumph, now served as a stark reminder of the enemies we had unwittingly made in our quest for success.

As the threats against our lives persisted,

it became increasingly clear that we were no longer safe in our own city. The relentless pursuit of our assailants left us on edge, constantly looking over our shoulders, never knowing when danger would strike next. In the face of such imminent peril, my priorities underwent a seismic shift—no longer did the allure of city contracts or financial gain hold any sway. The safety and well-being of my family became paramount, eclipsing all other concerns.

Driven by a primal instinct to protect those I loved, I resolved to extricate us from the perilous situation we found ourselves in. It was a decision born out of desperation, fueled by the urgent need to safeguard my family from the ever-present threat of violence.

Recalling a long-held desire to show my wife the world beyond our borders, I saw an opportunity amidst the chaos—a chance to flee the danger that loomed over us like a dark cloud. Though once hesitant to embark on such a journey, the shock and fear induced by our circumstances now spurred her to action, erasing any lingering doubts or reservations.

With a sense of urgency gripping us, we made preparations to leave the city, seeking refuge in the familiarity of her mother's home in the projects. There, we awaited the arrival of a crucial paycheck, the last vestige of our former life, before we embarked on our journey to safety.

As we counted down the days until our departure, I assumed the role of protector, a sentinel armed with nothing but a rifle and unwavering determination. Positioned by the window, I remained vigilant, ready to confront any threat that dared to encroach upon our sanctuary.

The tension in the air was palpable as two mysterious figures, clad in trench coats despite the warmth of the day, approached our doorstep. Instincts honed by years of military training kicked into high gear, my mind a wellspring of calculated readiness. At that moment, there was no room for hesitation or doubt only the primal instinct to defend my family at any cost.

With steely resolve, I braced myself for the inevitable confrontation, knowing full well that the lives of those who dared to threaten us hung in the balance. In that fleeting instant, fear gave way to a chilling sense of calm as I prepared to confront our would-be assailants with unwavering resolve.

Prepared to defend my family at all costs, I positioned myself strategically, my vantage point offering a clear line of sight to the impending threat. With unwavering resolve, I steeled myself for the confrontation that seemed inevitable, knowing that the lives of those who dared to threaten us hung in the balance.

As I braced to pull the trigger, my finger poised on the trigger, a sudden interruption shattered the tense silence. The arrival of the project security team, seemingly summoned by divine intervention, disrupted the assailants' sinister plans. Startled by the unexpected arrival of security, the would-be attackers hastily retreated, fleeing the scene in a desperate bid to escape apprehension.

Witnessing the swift intervention of security, a wave of relief washed over us, the gravity of the situation weighing heavy on our hearts. It was a stark reminder of the precariousness of our circumstances and the imminent danger that lurked in the shadows.

With the threat temporarily averted, we knew that our window of opportunity for escape was rapidly closing. The next morning, as if by fate, the awaited paycheck arrived, signaling our cue to depart. Without hesitation, we hastily packed our belongings and embarked on the journey to safety, California beckoning as a distant beacon of hope.

Despite our careful preparations, the

journey proved fraught with peril. The closer we drew to our destination, the more acutely aware we became of the ominous specter of pursuit. Armed but outnumbered, we navigated the treacherous terrain with a mounting sense of unease, every shadow seeming to harbor unseen dangers.

Arriving in California, we found ourselves ensnared in a web of surveillance, our every move monitored by unseen eyes. Exhausted and beleaguered, we were forced to abandon our plans, our family's safety taking precedence over any material possessions.

Faced with the harsh reality of our predicament, we made the difficult decision to redirect our journey, setting our sights on the distant sanctuary of Georgia. With each passing mile, the weight of our circumstances bore down upon us; our exhaustion was tempered only by the relentless determination to keep moving forward.

In the darkness of night, as we sought

refuge in transient lodgings, the safety of our children became our utmost priority. With vigilant eyes and weary hearts, we took turns standing guard, our restless vigil was a testament to the lengths; we would go through to protect those we held dear. Armed and vigilant, we pressed on, our resolve unyielding in the face of adversity.

As I recall, my mind began to brainstorm and immediately I started thinking, how could I turn six liabilities into six assets? How do I turn a housewife into a killing machine? How do I develop five kids to whereas, they can defend themselves? How do I transition my kids' mind to a point, where they are locking the doors behind themselves, looking back, and watching over themselves, whereas I do not have to? My method of operation was to join that the police department, myself. I thought about my wife joining the police department, also; so we could conduct a strict investigation to discover the motive of what happened to us.

We needed to know who was behind the contract hit. After my wife and I put in applications for the police department, she was hired, but I was not. She was accepted, but I was not because of my background of drug use. After that, I tried to go back into the military. Due to my age, I could not re-enlist, because my time had elapsed. My wife needed to re-enlisted. However, it was very difficult to convince her into going back into the military; but after the different attempts on our lives, she knew that there was no other option. She then re-enlisted in the military and that was the strategy I used to change the trajectory of our lives. I began to teach my wife karate. I taught my children karate, from the oldest to the youngest. I taught them how to defend themselves. I even walked with my wife to build up her endurance. We would get up every morning before she went to military and build up our endurance just in cased we had to fight. We never knew what was going to happen day to day until an attempt was made on our lives.

Therefore, we were preparing ourselves for battle. My wife became an expert in rifles. Well even in this day, she is still an expert in using her weaponry. She is able to use a pistol because of our ability to handle guns. I taught her how to quick draw. We were able to draw our weapons lightening fast. This is how I built my army and taught my family how to defend themselves.

Unfortunately, I never thought of how the attempts on our lives, hiding in hotels, and moving from one place to another would affect my family, mentally. I was focused on protecting them and teaching them how to defend themselves; until I did not realize, over and over this became trauma. Over the course of time, it began to wear and tear on us in every aspect: psychologically, mentally, emotionally, and physically. The PTSD began to wear on us, traumatically. Sadly, even though God brought us out of what appears to be an unscathed reality, in actuality the wounds were buried deep with our the corridors of our hearts. We did not escape this trauma unscathed, because now we have to deal with the discipline of our lives. It has seriously affected our family relationships in a negative manner, to this very day. For some of my family, the wounds of trauma has distorted the vision and reality of the past. There is nothing I can do about the past, regardless of our feelings. In spite of the methods of defense, I took my family to a safe place overseas with no income. I worked washing dishes, making sacrifices until l was hire into a better paying government job. I kept working and sacrificing in a foreign country, where we could not speak the language. I made sure they did not miss a meal. Even if I could not eat, they ate and they were always clothed, even when I wore the same clothes. It was challenging, but I was willing to do whatever I needed to do to protect my family, from our enemies. I suffered, endured, and made extreme sacrifices to protect my family. I pray that my family understands that in the midst of the perilous pursuit; my main objective back then, was to keep us together and alive!

Chapter 7
Finding Light in the Darkness

Amidst the uncertainty and fear that shadowed our every move, a chance encounter at a gas station heralded a glimmer of hope in the darkness. As I stepped out of the vehicle, weary and watchful, two strangers approached—a pair of black men whose warm smiles belied the gravity of our situation.

With a perceptiveness born of shared experience, they sensed the tension that hung heavy in the air, their concern evident as they inquired about the turmoil that had brought us to this moment. As I shared our harrowing tale of pursuit and fear, they listened intently, their empathy a balm to our troubled souls.

In a moment of shared understanding, they offered words of reassurance, their laughter cutting through the tension like a beacon of light. With unwavering confidence, they assured me that we possessed the strength and resilience to overcome the adversaries that dogged our every step.

Their words resonated deep within me, stirring a newfound sense of determination and resolve. In their laughter, I found solace, a reminder that even in the darkest times, the possibility of hope and salvation existed.

As we bid farewell to our newfound allies and resumed our journey, their words echoed in my mind, a guiding beacon of encouragement amidst the tumultuous sea of uncertainty. With renewed vigor, we pressed on, fortified by the unexpected kindness of strangers and the unshakable belief that we would find a way to break free from the shackles of fear that bound us.

Amidst the flickering fluorescent lights of the gas station, their words of wisdom resonated like a divine revelation. With a gentle yet resolute tone, they offered reassurance, urging me to cast aside the shackles of fear and embrace the certainty of victory. Their message, delivered with an otherworldly clarity, echoed in the recesses of my mind, a beacon of hope amidst the encroaching darkness.

To this very day, I hold fast to the belief that those two men were more than mere mortals—they were angels in disguise, sent to guide us through the tempest of uncertainty. Their words, a potent elixir for the soul, instilled within me the unwavering conviction that fear was the true adversary that must be vanquished before any battle could be waged.

Armed with this newfound clarity, we

continued our journey southward, the road stretching out before us like an uncharted path to salvation. With each passing mile, the weight of our burdens grew lighter, replaced by a renewed sense of purpose and determination.

Arriving in College Park, Georgia, we found sanctuary amidst the sprawling landscape of unfamiliar streets and unfamiliar faces. Yet, even as we sought solace in our newfound surroundings, the specter of danger loomed ever closer.

In the quiet serenity of my wife's workplace, the tendrils of fear tightened their grip once more. A stranger, bearing the weight of ominous intent, sought us out with a persistence that sent shivers down our spines.

In the face of this ominous threat, we knew that the time for action had come. With a steely resolve born of necessity, we resolved to take matters into our own hands—to protect ourselves and our loved ones from the encroaching darkness that threatened to engulf us.

When they came looking for her at her workplace, my wife, a dedicated nurse providing care to patients across Georgia, received a chilling warning from her employer. With a sense of foreboding settling over us like a heavy shroud, it became abundantly clear that danger still lurked ominously on the periphery. Despite our relocation to Georgia, the threat remained palpable, a shadowy specter that refused to be dispelled.

Realizing the gravity of our predicament, I resolved to take decisive action to safeguard our family against the looming threat. Setting into motion a plan born of necessity, we fortified our defenses, meticulously vetting every visitor to our home in a bid to discern friend from foe. Each face that crossed our threshold was scrutinized with a newfound wariness, every interaction fraught with the tension of impending danger.

In the midst of this turmoil, we made the difficult decision to uproot our lives once more, seeking refuge in the sanctuary of South Carolina. With meticulous planning and unwavering determination, we prepared to embark on a journey fraught with uncertainty yet infused with a glimmer of hope for a safer future.

As the pieces of our plan fell into place, my wife made the courageous decision to enlist in the military, a path that promised both security and stability in the face of adversity. With her departure for Fort Jackson looming on the horizon, I found myself tasked with the daunting responsibility of caring for our five children in her absence.

Left to navigate the challenges of single parenthood, I embraced the role with a fierce determination, drawing strength from the love and resilience that bound our family together. In the face of uncertainty, we stood united, our resolve unshakable in the face of adversity, as we braced ourselves for the tumultuous journey that lay ahead.

I assumed the role of caretaker for our children during her military training, shouldering the responsibility with unwavering dedication. When the time came for her to request her first duty station, she boldly opted for an overseas assignment, a decision that would alter the course of our lives in unforeseen ways. Thus, we remained stationed in South Carolina, biding our time until her training at Fort Sam Houston was complete.

With the end of her training drawing near, I embarked on a journey with our children, traversing the vast expanse of the country to reunite our family in Fort Sam Houston, Texas. The prospect of being together once more infused our hearts with hope and anticipation, the promise of a new chapter awaiting us on the horizon.

As we eagerly awaited her arrival, fate intervened once more, bestowing upon her military orders that would whisk us away to the distant shores of Germany. With a sense of serendipity that bordered on the miraculous, we found ourselves already in Germany when her orders came through, poised to embark on a new adventure as a united family.

Stepping foot on foreign soil, a palpable sense of liberation enveloped us, the weight of our past fears and uncertainties lifting like a veil in the crisp European air. For the first time in what felt like an eternity, we breathed deeply, savoring the sweet taste of freedom that had long eluded us. In the sanctuary of our newfound home, we felt untouchable, a world away from the dangers that had once haunted our every waking moment.

With the specter of danger now a distant memory, we embraced the opportunity to start anew, laying down roots in our adopted homeland. Inspired by a shared sense of faith and resilience, we embarked on a journey of spiritual renewal, opening our hearts and our homes to those seeking solace and community. In the hallowed halls of our humble church, we found purpose and belonging, a testament to the power of hope and perseverance in the face of adversity.

While my wife diligently served as a nurse in Landstuhl, Germany, tending to the needs of others with unwavering compassion, I found myself at a crossroads, grappling with the call to embark on a new journey—one that would ultimately lead me to open a church.

The genesis of this endeavor unfolded in a moment of divine intervention as I sat alone on the couch, contemplating my next steps in a foreign land. In the quiet solitude of our home, the Holy Spirit stirred within me, urging me to heed a higher calling.

In a leap of faith, I poured out my heart in prayer, grappling with the enormity of the task laid before me. "Lord," I beseeched, "I hear your call to open a church, but I am but a humble man without the means or resources to bring such a vision to fruition."

Yet, even in the depths of my uncertainty, I felt a reassuring presence enveloping me, a steadfast reminder that miracles can take root where faith abounds. With renewed determination, I set out to seek a venue for our fledgling congregation, guided by a sense of purpose that transcended earthly constraints.

Fortune smiled upon me when I stumbled upon an empty building nestled near my wife's workplace on the army post. Adjacent to it stood Romeo's Pizza, a beacon of familiarity in a sea of uncertainty. With trepidation mingled with hope, I approached the owner, whose demeanor exuded warmth and skepticism.

As I broached the subject of renting the space for our church, the owner's initial response was tinged with skepticism. "Do you have the means to afford it?" he inquired, his voice tinged with doubt.

In that moment, faced with the prospect of financial uncertainty, I chose honesty over embellishment. "No," I confessed, "I do not possess the financial means to meet your demands."

Yet, even as I spoke those words, I felt a quiet confidence welling up within me—a conviction that our shared vision was greater than any monetary barrier. With bated breath, I awaited his response, hoping against hope that he would see beyond the limitations of the material world and recognize the boundless potential that lay within our shared aspirations.

I explained that the Lord had instructed me to come, promising that he would grant me the building. Despite his skepticism, I left my contact information and departed for my wife's workplace. Upon returning home, I engaged in a heartfelt conversation with the Lord, expressing my feelings of foolishness for approaching the man with such an audacious request.

The following day, to my astonishment, the man appeared at my wife's workplace, urgently seeking my presence. Word had spread, and he was determined to locate me. When he finally found me, exhaustion etched upon his face, he pressed the keys into my hand. He confessed that he had been unable to sleep, tormented by his conscience. "Take these keys," he implored, "I cannot rest until this burden is lifted from my shoulders."

In a poignant moment of vulnerability, he revealed his battle with throat cancer and beseeched me to pray for him. Money, he declared, was of no consequence. All he desired was the solace of my prayers.

With the keys to the building now in my possession, we wasted no time in establishing our church—a humble sanctuary that would soon become a beacon of hope for our community. Within a matter of weeks, our congregation flourished, drawing newcomers with each passing Sunday.

Chapter 8

From Ashes to Refuge

From the moment our church doors swung open for the first time, it seemed providence had blessed us abundantly. Within a mere 30 days, our congregation swelled to over 30 fervent souls. We took up the mantle of shepherding this flock, and in our humble sanctuary, miracles unfolded. Lives were transformed, salvation found, and chains of bondage shattered.

News of the spiritual revival within our modest walls spread like wildfire, drawing seekers from far and wide, even across the breadth of Europe. Our quaint little church became a beacon of hope and renewal, attracting curious visitors from every corner. It was a sight to behold, witnessing the tapestry of humanity converging in pursuit of faith and redemption.

Meanwhile, amidst the spiritual fervor, I found myself navigating the earthly realm as a supervisor in a junkyard parts facility. Days were spent overseeing operations, but my heart remained tethered to the spiritual journey unfolding within our congregation.

Then came the fateful call that shattered the tranquil rhythm of our lives. Racing along the Autobahn, the world's fastest highway, I hurtled towards home with a sense of foreboding gnawing at my soul. Pulling onto Landstuhl Hill, the sight that greeted me was one of chaos and despair.

Government housing, where my family resided, was engulfed in turmoil. Fire trucks blared, military police stood vigilant, and the air crackled with tension. Racing through the throngs of onlookers, I felt a surge of panic grips my heart. The reason for the urgent summons became painfully clear.

Amidst the chaos, my mind raced, but one thought consumed me – the safety of my children. Ignoring the barricades and chaos, I dashed toward the heart of the commotion, desperately seeking their presence amidst the chaos. For at that moment, amidst the sirens and the chaos, nothing mattered more than ensuring the safety of my beloved family.

The aftermath of the fire was a scene straight out of a nightmare. Smoke billowed from the charred remains of what was once our home, tendrils of destruction weaving through the corridors of government housing. The stove left unattended, had become a malevolent agent of chaos, unleashing flames that devoured everything in their path. The damage, totaling a staggering $150,000, was a testament to the relentless fury of the inferno.

Amidst the chaotic scene, faces blurred together in a sea of concerned onlookers, their expressions reflecting the urgency of the moment. My heart pounded fiercely against my ribs as I scanned the throng, my eyes darting anxiously in search of any glimpse of my precious children. Every passing second felt like an eternity as fear clawed at my insides.

Then, amidst the tumult and cacophony, came the words I had been desperately yearning for – confirmation that my children were safe. Relief surged through me like a torrent, overwhelming the panic that had threatened to consume me moments before. It was as if a heavy burden had been lifted, replaced by an immense wave of gratitude that washed away the dread.

However, as the authorities guided us towards the back of a waiting police car, reality descended upon us with crushing force, like a relentless wave crashing upon the shore. Seated alongside my wife, the weight of our predicament settled upon our shoulders like an oppressive shroud. The tears glistening in her eyes mirrored the ache in my own heart, both of us grappling with the enormity of our situation.

Here we were, stranded in a foreign land, our sense of security shattered and stripped of everything we held dear. The uncertainty of what lay ahead loomed ominously, casting a shadow over our thoughts and dreams. In that moment, as we sat silently in the back of that police car, we clung to each other for support, united by the profound bond of love amidst the chaos of our circumstances.

In that cramped space, surrounded by the stark metal confines of the police car, the full extent of our loss hit us like a physical blow. Memories, cherished possessions, the very essence of our past – all reduced to ash and rubble. My wife's tears flowed freely, each droplet a silent testament to the depth of our despair.

Then amidst the chaos, a beacon of humanity emerged. Tony, a familiar face in the crowd, saw our anguish and cried out in solidarity. His voice pierced through the din, a rallying cry for compassion in the face of adversity. As his tears mingled with ours, the barriers of formality crumbled away, leaving only the rawness of shared grief.

It was then that a ray of hope pierced through the darkness. A colonel's wife, her compassion a guiding light in the chaos, intervened on our behalf. With unwavering resolve, she insisted that we be freed from the confines of the police car, offering sanctuary within the walls of her own home.

Guided by her gentle hand, we found ourselves welcomed into her abode, a refuge amidst the storm. She enveloped us with her husband i n a cocoon of empathy and understanding. As we sat there, surrounded by the warmth of their hospitality, we found solace in the simple act of human connection.

As the colonel's wife bustled about the kitchen, preparing tea with a kindness that seemed to belie the gravity of our situation, her husband, a stern figure in military regalia, loomed over us with a palpable air of disapproval. Anger simmered beneath the surface of his demeanor, his words laced with accusation and condemnation.

He wasted no time in venting his frustration, his voice a thunderous barrage of threats and recriminations. Each syllable was a dagger aimed at our already wounded hearts, promising repercussions that loomed ominously on the horizon. But amidst his tirade, I refused to cower. Though a civilian in the face of his military authority, I stood firm, a bulwark of defiance against the storm of his indignation.

For me, it was a matter of principle. Here was a man, supposed to be a protector of the people, lashing out with unchecked aggression towards me and my wi. The instinct to defend her honor, to confront him man to man, burned within me like a raging fire.

As tensions escalated, our exchange cracked with the intensity of two opposing forces on a collision course, and his wife intervened. With a courage born of empathy, she stepped between us, a beacon of reason in the midst of chaos. Soft yet resolute words carried the weight of righteousness as she pleaded for understanding and compassion in the face of tragedy.

Her insistence, a resolute defense of our plight, became an impenetrable shield against the relentless onslaught of his fury. Each word she spoke echoed with conviction, a steadfast resolve that seemed to chip away at the walls of his anger. As she stood her ground, unwavering in her determination, a remarkable transformation took place. His aggressive stance softened, his features gradually relaxing into a begrudging acceptance of her unwavering wisdom.

Yet, it was not solely her words that offered solace in our darkest hour. No, it was the profound kindness radiating from every line of her face, every gesture of her being. The warmth of her embrace enveloped us as she sat with us on the floor, her presence a soothing balm to our wounded spirits. At that moment, it felt as though God Himself had sent this angel of mercy to watch over us and shield us from the world's harshness.

Her compassion, a beacon of light amidst the shadows, illuminated the path forward, instilling a glimmer of hope amidst the despair within us. As we gazed into her eyes, we found not just solace but a renewed sense of strength to face whatever trials lay ahead. In her presence, we discovered the true essence of humanity – a boundless capacity for love and empathy that transcended the barriers of language and circumstance.

As she spoke to her husband, her voice was a gentle persuasion that softened the hard edges of his resolve, and a sense of relief washed over us. For in her, we found an ally and a lifeline, someone who understood the depth of our loss and was determined to help us rebuild.

In her, we found a protector and a minister of grace, guiding us through the darkness with the light of her compassion. As we sat together, enveloped in her embrace, we knew that no matter the challenges ahead, we would not face them alone.

In mere days, we found ourselves whisked away into a sprawling six-bedroom palace, a place so breathtakingly beautiful that it felt like stepping into a dream. The sheer grandeur of it all overwhelmed us – each room was a sanctuary meticulously designed for every member of our family. It was a haven amidst the chaos, a sanctuary we never dared imagine.

As we settled into our new home, the kindness of strangers continued to astound us. Vouchers in hand, we ventured to DRMO, where we were met with an abundance of military furniture and bedding, each piece a symbol of support and care from a community we had yet to fully comprehend. Brand new carpeting adorned every inch of our palace, transforming it into a haven of warmth and comfort.

Then came the generosity of the government, a lifeline extended just when we needed it most. Thousands upon thousands of dollars poured in, a financial reprieve that seemed almost too good to be true. But it didn't stop there – friends from our past, from one of our old churches, rallied around us, offering not just money but clothes, toiletries, and every essential we could possibly need. Their generosity was a beacon of hope in our darkest hour.

But amidst the blessings, there was also heartache. Article 15 loomed over my wife, a burden that weighed heavily on our shoulders, especially being so far from home with our children. The decision to leave Germany was painful, made even more so by the tearful farewells of our beloved church community. Their anguish mirrored our own, their pleas for us to stay echoing in our ears long after we departed.

In the end, despite their desperate entreaties, I found myself powerless to change my wife's decision. It was a choice borne of necessity, tinged with sorrow and regret. As we left behind the only home we had ever known overseas, our hearts ached with the bittersweet realization that sometimes, even the most well-meaning gestures cannot mend what has been broken.

Chapter 9

Navigating Betrayal, Bounty, and Boundless Determination

My wife longed to escape, her heart heavy with the weight of hurt and humiliation. The pain of betrayal lingered like a bitter taste in her mouth, pushing her to flee from the place that had brought her so much anguish. With resolve in her eyes and determination in her heart, she made the decision to return home to Georgia, seeking solace in familiar surroundings.

But as we embarked on their journey back to the United States, our pockets were heavy with the unexpected bounty of thousands of dollars. It was a small comfort in the face of uncertainty, a lifeline we clung to as we navigated the complexities of starting anew. Yet, despite the financial cushion, our path was fraught with challenges, particularly as our children approached the precipice of adulthood.

With college and school looming on the horizon for our children, practicality dictated our next steps. Three different vehicles became a necessity, each purchase a reminder of the sacrifices made for the ones we loved. Yet, even with the weight of responsibility bearing down upon us, the burden of finding shelter remained.

Our temporary refuge became a hotel in the bustling city of Atlanta, a place of refuge that came at a steep cost. Every night spent within its walls served as a stark reminder of the precariousness of our situation, the urgency to carve out a new existence palpable in every moment.

But amidst the chaos and uncertainty, a flicker of hope emerged. In the depths of our struggle, an idea took root – a beacon of possibility in an otherwise bleak landscape. It was a spark of innovation, a glimmer of light in the darkness, offering a glimpse of a future filled with promise and potential.

I proposed a solution born out of desperation and determination: let's buy a trailer and seek refuge in Alabama, where the cost of living is more affordable. With hope flickering like a fragile flame, we made the bold decision to invest in 40 acres of land, a symbol of our unwavering commitment to building a new life from the ashes of our past. Though our initial plan was to purchase the entire plot, financial constraints forced us to settle for 20 acres in Randolph County, Alabama.

Leaving behind the confines of the hotel, where each day felt like a race against time and dwindling resources, we embarked on the journey to our new home. It was a leap of faith, a desperate gamble made in the eleventh hour. As we crossed state lines into Alabama, the weight of uncertainty bore down upon us, each mile marking a step closer to a future filled with unknowns.

Settling into our humble trailer, I poured every ounce of my being into transforming it into a sanctuary where we could find respite from the storms that raged outside. Every nail hammered, every board secured was a testament to our resilience, a reminder that we refused to be defeated even in the face of adversity.

But a chilling realization dawned upon us amidst the sweat and toil of rebuilding our lives. In the quiet of the evening, as I returned home weary from a day's labor, I found my wife sitting on the couch, her eyes glazed with disbelief. The air hung heavy with tension as she uttered those fateful words, her voice trembling with fear and uncertainty. "Harold," she whispered, "they're still looking for us."

Five long years had passed, yet the specter of danger still loomed over us like a dark cloud. My wife's words cut through the tranquility of our newfound sanctuary, her voice heavy with worry and apprehension. It wasn't just the mere fact that people were asking about us; it was the sinister undertones, the unspoken threats that hung in the air like a palpable menace. She knew, deep down, that our peace was but a fragile illusion, shattered by the relentless pursuit of those who sought to do us harm.

So, here we were, nestled in the quiet solitude of our trailer, surrounded by acres of untamed beauty that we called our own. The land stretched out before us like a canvas of dreams, each stream and meadow a testament to the freedom we had fought so hard to attain. In the gentle embrace of nature, we found solace, a respite from the chaos that seemed to follow us at every turn.

But our idyllic existence was short-lived, shattered by the harsh reality of our circumstances. We faced the painful truth with a heavy heart: we were no longer safe here. The very land that had once offered us sanctuary now felt like a prison, its beauty tainted by the looming threat of danger.

As we hastily packed our belongings into the confines of our SUV, the weight of uncertainty bore down upon us. Every item we stowed away was a reminder of the life we were leaving behind, a stark testament to the harsh realities of our existence. Yet, amidst the chaos, there was a glimmer of hope – a desperate attempt to make sense of the madness that had engulfed us.

With trembling hands, I dialed the familiar number, hoping against hope for some semblance of answers. Was it all just a cruel hoax, or were we truly in danger? The voice on the other end offered no solace or reassurance – only the cold, hard truth that our enemies were closer than we had ever imagined. Therefore, with a heavy heart and a sense of foreboding, we set out once more into the unknown, leaving behind the echoes of our shattered dreams in the quiet stillness of our abandoned home.

The hotel room felt suffocating, the weight of uncertainty pressing down on us like a heavy blanket. As I demanded answers from the hotel staff, their vague responses offered little comfort, only serving to deepen the sense of dread that hung in the air like a thick fog. It was a chilling realization that we were not safe here, that danger lurked just beyond the walls of our temporary refuge.

With every passing minute, the threat drew closer, a menacing shadow looming ever larger on the horizon. There was no time to waste, no luxury of deliberation – we had to act, and we had to act fast. In a flurry of frantic activity, we gathered our belongings, each item a lifeline in the face of imminent danger. The children's clothes, their school supplies, every shred of paperwork that held even the slightest semblance of importance – nothing was left behind as we hastily packed our lives into the confines of our vehicle.

Then without a moment's hesitation, we were on the move once more, the road stretching out before us like a path to the unknown. But amidst the chaos, there was a flicker of determination in my wife's eyes, a silent resolve that spoke volumes. Though separated by oceans and continents, our bond remained unbroken, our shared goal driving us forward in the face of adversity.

With a heavy heart, I made the difficult decision to leave my wife behind, her safety entrusted to the care of a trusted friend. It was a sacrifice borne out of necessity, a temporary separation in service of a greater purpose. As I embarked on yet another journey overseas, the weight of responsibility hung heavy on my shoulders, each step forward a testament to the lengths we would go to protect our family.

But even in the darkest of moments, there was a glimmer of hope – a belief that no matter the obstacles we faced, we would emerge stronger and more resilient than before. So with determination in our hearts and the promise of a brighter future on the horizon, we pressed on, ready to face whatever challenges lay ahead.

As I journeyed back overseas in search of a new beginning, the landscape of familiarity had shifted beneath my feet. The once-thriving churches that had been my pillars of support now stood empty and desolate, their halls echoing with the ghosts of bygone congregations. Yet amidst the rubble of broken dreams, a beacon of hope emerged in the form of an old acquaintance – a minister whose kindness would become my lifeline in a sea of uncertainty.

With open arms, he welcomed me into his home, a refuge amidst the storm of upheaval. It was a gesture of generosity that touched me to the core, a reminder that even in the darkest of times, there are still rays of light to guide us through the darkness. As he handed me the keys to one of his vehicles, a symbol of newfound freedom, I couldn't help but feel a surge of gratitude for this unexpected blessing.

"It's impossible to navigate Europe without a vehicle," he insisted, his voice filled with conviction. "Take this van, and may it serve you well on your journey."

In the warmth of his home, surrounded by the laughter of his family, I found solace in the midst of chaos. It was a temporary respite, a fleeting moment of peace before the harsh realities of life came crashing back in.

But even as I struggled to find my footing in this unfamiliar land, I refused to succumb to despair. With determination in my heart, I sought out whatever employment I could find, no task too humble, no job too menial. Although washing dishes may have seemed like a small victory to some, to me, it was a sign of progress, a step forward on the path to rebuilding my life.

In the midst of my newfound stability, I found myself drawn to a church where my benefactor and his wife worshipped. It was a sanctuary of faith and fellowship, a place where I could find solace in the company of kindred spirits. But even within its hallowed halls, whispers of discord lingered, reminders of the fragile nature of human relationships.

The minister who had extended his hand in friendship had a past marred by mistakes, and his fall from grace was a stain on his reputation. Yet, despite his flaws, I couldn't help but admire his resilience and his unwavering commitment to serving others in spite of his own shortcomings.

As the congregation grappled with the complexities of forgiveness and redemption, I couldn't help but wonder about the true nature of grace – a concept as elusive as it was profound. As I bore witness to the inner turmoil of those around me, I couldn't help but reflect on my journey toward healing and redemption.

CHAPTER 10
Family, Faith, and Finding Purpose

No matter how much we try to prepare, there's one facet of life that remains elusive: the insidious grip of PTSD. Despite the positive changes unfolding in my life, the trauma I endured refused to loosen its hold, manifesting itself in the relentless presence of PTSD.

PTSD is a silent assailant that infiltrates the very essence of one's being, reshaping their perceptions and responses to the world around them. Its effects are subtle yet profound, often hidden beneath the veneer of normalcy until familiarity unveils the stark contrast in behavior.

It wasn't until I intimately knew my family that I began to discern the quiet struggles they bore from the threats upon their lives. The once carefree demeanor of my children had undergone a transformation, their innocence marred by the invisible scars of trauma.

Despite their enduring beauty and innate kindness, it was evident that they grappled with the burden of PTSD. How does a parent navigate the delicate terrain of raising children whose innocence has been tainted by fear? How does one explain the necessity of silence amidst the cacophony of danger or deny them the simple joys of play when the specter of uncertainty looms overhead?

Every "hush" uttered in response to a noise, every denial of outdoor adventures, is infused with the weight of a parent's unspoken anguish, borne from the relentless vigilance demanded by their circumstances. In those moments of enforced stillness, one can't help but feel the palpable tension in the air, a chilling reminder of the ever- present threat that refuses to loosen its grip.

In the embroidery of raising kids, amidst the everyday bumps and scrapes that come with childhood, there was a tricky balance over- shadowed by the looming threat of being kicked out of Europe.

As parents, we know that kids, no matter where they are, will inevitably find themselves in some mischief. But our situation was far from normal. We were on thin ice, with our stay in Europe at risk due to a range of events—from a big fire at a government building to the usual antics of our children.

The seriousness of our situation weighed heavily on us. Every day felt like walking a tightrope between protecting our kids and keeping our fragile lives together. The thought that our children's typical kid stuff could uproot us from the only stability we had left haunted us constantly.

I can't bear to think about what our kids went through in the middle of such tough times. Their innocence, once a source of joy, now reminded us of the danger we were all in. We weren't just trying to help them grow up; we were trying to shield them from the very real threat that hung over our heads.

Our days were a whirlwind of survival, with every stern word and punishment tinged with desperation. We wrestled with guilt for putting our kids through trials they shouldn't have faced at such a young age, knowing that our survival depended on them staying strong with us.

In the face of adversity, our roles as parents and protectors blurred together as we navigated through unfamiliar territory out of sheer necessity. Our love for our kids kept us grounded when things got tough and pushed us forward when we felt like giving up.

Despite the challenges we faced, my children have grown into genuinely kind-hearted individuals. Even though occasional conflicts may arise even now, my love for them remains unwavering. I hold them in the highest regard, recognizing the profound impact of PTSD on our lives.

Understanding the depth of that impact has been an eye-opening journey. It's a reality I've come to accept—a toll that had to be paid, even though its weight remained invisible to others.

No one could perceive the silent struggles I endured. No one could fathom the anguish that gnawed at me when my children ventured out into the world, their safety a constant source of concern.

The unseen burden of a father haunted by the looming threat of violence against his family is a heavy one to bear. The thought of harm befalling my offspring was a specter that loomed over every moment, casting a shadow over the simple joys of parenthood.

Navigating life with my family was akin to juggling a multitude of personalities, each as unique as they were diverse. With five distinct children, each with their own set of quirks and characteristics, and then there was my wife, with her individuality adding another layer of complexity to our dynamic. It was a delicate dance, one that required constant vigilance and adaptability.

Every day presented new challenges as I grappled not only with the external threats looming over us but also with the internal struggles that remained hidden from view. The weight of responsibility bore down on me, leaving me in a perpetual state of tension and anxiety. Why did Daddy seem distant? Why did Daddy's temper flare at the slightest provocation? These were questions that lingered in the minds of my loved ones, born from a lack of understanding of the burdens I carried.

The invisible wounds I bore ran deep, their impact reverberating within the confines of my own being. Though unseen, they were keenly felt —a constant reminder of the sacrifices made in the name of preserving our family's safety and well- being.

To my family, I extend my sincerest apologies for any pain or confusion my actions may have caused. Every decision every sacrifice, was made with the sole intention of safeguarding the ones I hold most dear. Yet, I acknowledge that my efforts may have inadvertently caused hurt or resentment.

I harbor no bitterness, only a profound sense of remorse for any distress I may have caused. If there are wounds that linger, I understand, and I humbly ask for forgiveness. My only hope is that, in time, understanding and healing may pave the way for reconciliation and peace within our family.

Returning to the discussion left unfinished in the previous chapter, the focus was on the minister. Despite his current role within the church, his past was marred by less-than-favorable circumstances. The community harbored grievances against him, urging me to take action. Allegations surfaced suggesting inappropriate conduct with a young woman, despite his marital status, which led to doubts about his suitability for the ministry within our congregation. In response, I reasoned with them, explaining that the reported incident occurred before his affiliation with our church.

The situation escalated when they presented me with an ultimatum: either remove the minister, or they would withdraw eight members along with the vital TAD funding that sustained our church's operations. Undeterred by their threats, I stood firm in my conviction, refusing to cast judgment on the minister for transgressions predating his commitment to our congregation and his renewed faith in the Lord.

I emphasized the importance of redemption and forgiveness, recognizing the transformative power of spiritual renewal. This man, once troubled by his past, had undergone a profound change, embodying the essence of a new creation in Christ. His gesture of goodwill didn't go unnoticed; he welcomed me into his home, provided me with transportation, and extended his care and support during my time in Germany.

This experience taught me a valuable lesson: people are not disposable commodities to be discarded at the whim of others' judgments. The minister, despite his flaws, played a pivotal role in my life, offering me refuge and opportunities that ultimately shaped my journey. It reinforced the principle that compassion and understanding should prevail over the desire for retribution.

Furthermore, the minister's kindness extended beyond our personal interactions; he introduced me to his church community, which sadly faced persecution, compelling them to flee the country. This added layer of adversity underscored the fragility of human connections and the resilience required to navigate life's challenges.

The pastors of the church I was invited to face the harsh reality of having to flee the country, leaving behind a congregation in need of guidance and support. In a remarkable turn of events, I found myself thrust into a leadership role, assuming the responsibilities of an assistant pastor under the oversight of a bishop. Suddenly, I was at the helm of a church community, entrusted with shepherding its members through tumultuous times.

As fate would have it, the bishop, too, was compelled to depart, leaving behind an apartment that he generously passed on to me. It was nothing short of a miracle, a testament to the unforeseen blessings that often arise from adversity.

With swift determination, I embraced my newfound role as pastor, stepping into the shoes of those who had gone before me. Within mere months of returning to Europe, I found myself at the helm of a thriving congregation, brimming with eager souls seeking solace and spiritual guidance.

The support extended to me by the kind- hearted individuals who crossed my path was immeasurable. No longer confined to living in their homes, I now had a vehicle at my disposal, a job to sustain us, and a roof over our heads. The pieces of the puzzle were falling into place, paving the way for the long-awaited reunion with my wife and family.

As they arrived in Europe, my wife seamlessly transitioned into her role as co-pastor, her presence a source of strength and unity. Despite never having received our official licenses, our shared commitment to ministry and the guidance we received through ministerial classes prepared us for the journey ahead.

Together, we embarked on a new chapter, fortified by faith and buoyed by the unwavering support of our newfound community. It was a testament to the transformative power of resilience, perseverance, and the boundless grace of God.

Following our licensing by Bishop Lee H. Evans in Europe, we underwent rigorous training and received our official paperwork, marking the beginning of our formal ministry journey on the continent. However, our path was not without its twists and turns.

Initially, we found ourselves settled at a church where we served diligently for a period. Yet, an invitation from another congregation to pastor their church presented itself, and we accepted the opportunity, embracing the challenge with open hearts.

However, a lingering sense of unease gnawed at us despite our dedication to the church we were leading. We longed for the autonomy and sense of ownership that comes with shepherding our own congregation, much like we had done at the outset of our journey in Europe.

Eventually, our persistence bore fruit, and we were blessed with the opportunity to establish our own church. To our amazement, the church seemed to flourish overnight, drawing in members from near and far, eager to partake in the community we had fostered.

As our church grew, so did our responsibilities beyond the pulpit. My wife, now a European civilian, found fulfillment in her role at a childcare development center while honing her culinary skills. She secured employment as a wage-grade worker for the government, a position I, too, held, cementing our ties to the community and providing stability alongside our pastoral duties.

In this newfound equilibrium of government employment and pastoral ministry, we found a sense of fulfillment and purpose, our professional endeavors intertwining seamlessly with our spiritual calling. Together, we embarked on a journey of service and devotion, guided by faith and a shared commitment to making a positive impact on the lives of those around us.

Chapter 11

The Dawn of Hope

Europe greeted us once again; five years had passed since our last footsteps echoed through its streets. As I stand here, the familiarity of it all washes over me like a comforting wave. It's as if time had circled back, returning us to our starting point.

Life has been kind to us in these years. We have ascended to a place of comfort and prosperity. Our residence now graces the grandeur of the Royal, a testament to our journey from humble beginnings to esteemed status. But it's not just the luxury of our abode that speaks volumes; it's the symbolism it carries, a marker of our triumph over adversity.

In this foreign land, we have carved out our own sanctuary, a church where the doors swing wide for all who seek solace. It's a peculiar sight— a civilian pastor tending to the spiritual needs of military personnel. Yet, here we stand, bridging the gap between two worlds, our voices resonating within the walls as we preach words of hope and salvation.

Our congregation burgeons with each passing day, a testament to the enthusiasm and passion that pulse within us. But with growth comes a clamor, a cacophony of voices raised in praise and worship that spills beyond the confines of our sanctuary.

We have become too loud for our own quarters, a realization that prompts a bittersweet move. In His infinite wisdom, God guides us across the threshold, leading us to civilian housing nestled within the heart of the government domain. It's a transition that feels like coming full circle, a return of property to its rightful owners—the Germans.

As we settle into our new surroundings, I can't help but feel a sense of déjà vu. Here we are, back where we started, yet infinitely changed by the journey that brought us here. The echoes of home reverberate through these halls, reminding us of the trials we have overcome and the blessings we have been bestowed. Amidst it all, we stand, ready to embrace whatever lies ahead on this new chapter of our European odyssey.

Settling into our new home on the airbase, we found ourselves in the middle of something quite interesting. Outside our church, the German government was busy testing Mercedes Benz cars. It was quite a sight, with technicians putting these vehicles through their paces while we conducted our services inside.

After church, everyone would spill out to watch the tests. It was fascinating to see how they tested the cars, especially with water and ice in front of us. But amidst all this excitement, we had our jobs to focus on. Both my wife and I were working for the government now. Undoubtedly, these were good jobs, but they came with their challenges.

Working in government jobs meant dealing with a lot of rules and bureaucracy. It wasn't always easy, and there were times when we faced obstacles that made things difficult.

Still, we did not let that deter us. Our faith kept us going, strengthening us even when things got tough. With the support of our church community, we knew we could overcome any challenge that came our way.

Life on the airbase was full of contrasts. From the roar of engines during car tests to the quiet moments of worship in our church, it was a place where different worlds collided. Through it all, we remained determined to make the most of our new life, knowing that each obstacle was just another opportunity to grow and learn.

The competition for these government

jobs was fierce. Those who had settled in Germany, marrying locals, were incredibly determined to secure these positions. They saw them as jobs and tickets to stability and prosperity. But amidst the allure of these roles; there lurked a darker reality— a reality tinged with racial tensions and sabotage.

In my job, I faced challenges from these underlying tensions. People sought to undermine my work, driven by prejudice and a desire to see me fail. Every day became a battle, a struggle to prove myself in adversity.

God had blessed me with intelligence and resilience. I refused to be deterred by the obstacles thrown my way. Instead, I devised a strategy to outsmart my detractors. I would present my work to the supervisor each evening, ensuring it was thoroughly checked and signed off. This way, when the sabotage inevitably occurred overnight, there was tangible evidence of foul play.

It was a constant game of cat and mouse,

but I refused to be the mouse. Armed with faith and determination, I confronted each challenge head- on, refusing to let the machinations of others dictate my destiny. As I persevered through the trials, I found solace in knowing that God was by my side, guiding me through the stormy seas of prejudice and adversity.

As tensions escalated in my workplace, the situation drew attention from authorities back in Texas. Reports of racial slurs and attempts to replace us with individuals who did not share our background reached the ears of government officials. It was a stark reminder of the discrimination we faced, a bitter pill to swallow as we fought to retain our livelihoods.

Meanwhile, at our church, we found ourselves amid a stark contrast. The Carpentry, our new sanctuary, stood as a beacon of hope and unity —a sprawling edifice capable of accommodating thousands. Yet, despite its grandeur, our congregation remained humble in size, numbering only a fraction of its capacity.

It was a peculiar irony to preach within the vast expanse of our new church, knowing that its halls could echo with the voices of thousands, while outside those walls, I battled against prejudice and injustice in my workplace. Even as I stood before the congregation, delivering messages of faith and resilience, the weight of my struggles pressed heavily upon me.

In those preaching moments, I found solace and strength, drawing inspiration from the unwavering faith of those gathered before me. Their presence reminded me that despite our trials, we were not alone. Together, we stood as a testament to the power of community and resilience, refusing to be silenced by the injustices that sought to divide us.

As I spoke, the words flowed from my lips, imbued with a sense of conviction and determination. For in that sacred space, amidst the grandeur of the Carpentry, we found refuge from the storms of prejudice and discrimination, united in our pursuit of justice and equality.

As I stood before the congregation, preparing to deliver my sermon, a tumult of emotions surged within me. The weight of the injustices faced in my workplace bore down on my spirit, mingling with the fervent prayers I offered up for those in need.

Addressing the congregation, I spoke of the trials and tribulations that many endured, assuring them that God would not turn a blind eye to their suffering. "For those who seek to bring trouble upon you," I proclaimed, "God's righteous fire will rain down upon them."

In that moment, as the words left my lips, a remarkable turn of events unfolded. My deacon, a stalwart soldier who prided himself on punctuality, arrived late—an unprecedented occurrence. His solemn demeanor as he approached me spoke volumes before he even uttered a word.

Seated beside me, he delivered news that sent shivers down my spine. "Where you work," he began, his voice heavy with gravity, "is engulfed in flames. Fire trucks swarmed the area, and I was delayed in reaching church as I waited for them to clear the way."

It was a revelation that resonated deeply within me, a stark reminder of the divine protection that encircled us even amid adversity. In that moment, I was reminded of the immutable truth that God's providence remains steadfast no matter where we find ourselves.

With a renewed sense of faith and purpose, I rose to deliver my sermon, encouraged by the assurance that God would indeed watch over His own. As the congregation listened intently, I shared the miraculous revelation, emphasizing that His protection would never waver, even in the face of raging fires.

For in that sacred space, amidst the flickering candles and hushed whispers of prayer, we found solace in the knowledge that no trial was too great, no challenge too daunting, for the Almighty was ever-present, guiding us through the darkest of nights into the radiant dawn of His grace.

As I stood there recounting the trials and triumphs of my journey, I couldn't help but be overwhelmed by the profound sense of gratitude and awe that filled my heart. God had remained faithful through every adversity and challenge, a steadfast guardian shielding my family and me from harm.

Reflecting on the past decade spent in Europe, I marveled at the countless doors that had been flung open by divine providence. From establishing our church to navigating government employment's intricacies, each opportunity had been a testament to God's unwavering grace.

Amidst the blessings, a shadow of uncertainty lingered—a longing in my wife's heart to return home. Despite the years of toil and triumphs, she yearned for the familiar embrace of our homeland. Her resolve was unyielding, her desire to depart from Europe unshakeable.

Therefore with heavy hearts, we made the decision to bid farewell to the land that had become our second home. As we embarked on the journey back, I could not help but ponder the lessons learned, the trials endured, and the faith that had sustained us through it all.

This book, I realized was more than just a recounting of personal experiences; it was a testament to the reality of spiritual warfare. From the very moment of my birth, the devil had sought to extinguish the flame of my existence, from the umbilical cord wrapped around my neck to the trials I faced in adulthood.

Yet, through it all, God remained a beacon of hope, guiding us through the darkest nights and into the light of His eternal love. As I penned these words, I did so to share my story and remind pastors everywhere that the battle against evil is accurate, and only through unwavering faith and divine protection can we hope to emerge victorious.

As I continued to reflect on the trials and tribulations that had marked my journey, memories of darker days resurfaced, haunting reminders of the relentless assaults waged by the enemy. From a tender age, I had been thrust into a world tainted by violence and depravity, forced to confront the rawness and brutality of existence.

At just nine years old, I found myself crafting makeshift weapons—zip guns—to safeguard my family in a world where danger lurked around every corner. I had seen the horror of humanity, the seething underbelly of society laid bare before me, and I had no choice but to navigate its treacherous waters alone.

As I matured, the specter of violence continued to loom large, casting its shadow over my life. I witnessed my beloved wife fall victim to a senseless shooting—a moment of despair that threatened to consume me whole. Yet, even in my darkest hour, God's guiding hand was ever-present, leading me through the labyrinth of alleyways, evading capture, and preserving my sanity amidst the chaos.

There were moments when I teetered on the brink of darkness when the allure of revenge and retribution beckoned like a siren's call. Yet, in those moments of temptation, God's voice whispered softly, urging me to remain steadfast in His grace.

There are parts of my story that I cannot bring myself to recount, horrors too harrowing to be spoken aloud. I cannot describe the countless times the enemy sought to snuff out my life, nor the countless battles fought in the shadows to protect those I held dear.

But through it all, God's light shone brightest in the darkest of hours, transforming me from a mere survivor into a warrior—a sentinel standing guard against the encroaching darkness. As I penned these words, I did so not to glorify violence or myself but to bear witness to the unfathomable depths of God's mercy and the resilience of the human spirit in the face of unspeakable evil.

The tumultuous journey of my life, from the battlegrounds of war to the depths of addiction, served as a crucible through which God's grace and redemption flowed. In the crucible of military conflict, amidst the chaos of Operation Desert Storm and Operation Desert Shield, I witnessed the transformative power of faith unfold.

As a soldier, I had experienced the horrors of war firsthand, grappling with the weight of mortality and the fragility of human existence. Yet, it was in those darkest moments that God's divine purpose became manifest. Through a series of remarkable twists of fate, I found myself positioned in the heart of the battlefield, not as a warrior but as a vessel of God's love and compassion.

Baptizing soldiers before they embarked on their perilous journey into the desert sands, I became acutely aware of the gravity of my calling. These were not just men and women in uniform— they were someone's sons and daughters, entrusted into my care by a higher power. With each baptism, I bore witness to the transformative power of faith, as fear gave way to hope and despair yielded to divine assurance.

Beside me stood my wife, a pillar of strength and compassion, as she assumed the role of mother to soldiers far from home. Together, we nurtured and guided these young men and women, offering them solace and support in the midst of uncertainty and danger.

It wasn't until years later that the full magnitude of our mission became clear to me. We weren't just providing spiritual guidance; we were serving as surrogate parents to a generation of warriors, instilling in them the values of faith, perseverance, and resilience.

In the face of imminent danger and death, these soldiers found refuge in the arms of the Lord, surrendering their lives to His divine will. Through the threat of war, they discovered the eternal peace that only God could provide, finding solace in the knowledge that they were never alone, that He who watches over them neither slumbers nor sleeps.

As I look back on those tumultuous years, I am humbled by the realization that God had strategically placed us amid adversity to be beacons of hope and agents of His love. For in the crucible of conflict, amidst the specter of death, His light shone brightest, illuminating the path to salvation and eternal life.

They realized how death could come at any time, how they were put in harm's way just by being American soldiers. This book is to remind pastors that they don't place themselves. This book is to remind pastors that God knows where He needs you to be. God will let you go through hell for you to lead others to heaven. He would allow the evil. He will allow you to go through the sewers of life so that you can bring His children through, pull them out of the sewers of life, fight for them, and defend them.

Now, I'm going to go back just for a moment to my job. When I was standing up, I said, "God will rain fire down on the people that mess over His children." As my deacon began to explain, the place was on fire. I realized at that very second that my job was on fire. I realized the power of life and death is in the tongue. I realized that God has not left His children alone. God has not left His children to fend for themselves. But God Himself is fighting right now, even though there are school shootings, even though there are people who are coming into the church and killing the church people. Sadly, they think that God told them to do it.

This earth has turned, and the pastors need to know, even though they're going through being shot at and having to lock the church doors, that God has not turned His back on His church. He is equipping His people and pulling people from the gutter. He is pulling people from the trenches. He is pulling people from the trash. He is bringing them out and making them fathers and mothers, pastors, and all the people who don't know the way. He has allowed them to go through hell so that they can help people to get to heaven. This book is to remind pastors that they are not their own. But they are bought and paid for with the blood of Jesus. We are bought. We are servants of the highest God. God places us in these positions, in these foreign countries, and in these trenches to be able to save others. Some of the pastors have lost families.

Out of all that I have been through, I am no longer with my family. Some of us have lost our families in the trenches, but it's worth it. Some of us have lost time and lost money. Some of us would have already been millionaires, but we have lost things for Christ. But God is yet in control, and we still have to trust God no matter what position we find ourselves in. Right now, I'm in a position where I can only pray for my family.

Who knows what my situation entails? The severity of what I've been through, death after death after death threats? Death after death attempts have been done to my five children and what has been done to my wife. Who knows the tiredness inside? Who knows that I've had enough of witnessing what she has gone through? This book is to save other pastors and to know that your walk is not easy. That you still have to go on. You still have to be the father. You still have to be an Abraham leading the flock. You still have to work at helping others while you, yourself are wounded. While you and yourself feel like you have been stepped on and forgotten about. This book is to encourage pastors that there is a better day. There's a better day coming. I believe a better day is coming on earth and even in heaven, eternally. So pastors let this book heal you no matter what you maybe going through. Servants of the Highest God, no matter what you are going through right now, be courageous! Go through it. There is a better day coming. There is a day that God will vindicate you and show that he was always with you.

www.ingramcontent.com/pod-product-compliance
Lightning Source LLC
Chambersburg PA
CBHW070105080526
44586CB00013B/1189